RUBANK EDUCATIONAL LIBRARY No. 14

RUBANK
INTERMEDIATE
Method

BASSOON

H. VOXMAN

A FOLLOW UP COURSE FOR INDIVIDUAL OR LIKE-INSTRUMENT CLASS INSTRUCTION

RUBANK
HAL•LEONARD
CORPORATION
7777 W. Bluemound Rd. P.O. Box 13819 Milwaukee, WI 53213

Review of Fundamental Rhythms

Play the following exercises slowly and with a full tone.

Copyright MCMXLVII by Rubank, Inc., Chicago, Ill.
International Copyright Secured

TRIPLET ETUDE

Do not hurry the triplets. Play with a full tone.

ALLA BREVE (Cut time)

DOTTED QUARTERS AND EIGHTHS

Be sure the eighth note following the dotted quarter note begins on time.

DOTTED HALVES AND QUARTERS IN ¢

CHROMATIC SCALE

Check fingerings

Principal Dynamic Marks Used in Music

Pianissimo... *pp* very soft   Fortissimo.. *ff* very loud
Piano ...... *p* soft   Forte...... *f* loud
Mezzo Piano. *mp* moderately soft.   Mezzo Forte. *mf* moderately loud.

The ability to play the range of your instrument at the various dynamic levels is a highly necessary one. Be sure that the proper pitch and quality are not sacrificed. *Listen carefully.*

Do not let the tones vary from the dynamic indicated.

Practice the following exercise on different notes of the scale.

STUDY IN DYNAMIC CONTRAST

Dynamic Gradations

Crescendo *(cresc.)* ⟨ gradually louder.   Diminuendo *(dim.)* ⟩ gradually softer.

Be sure the increase or decrease in loudness is gradual, not in steps; thus ⟨ , not ⟨

Always give first consideration to tone quality and intonation.

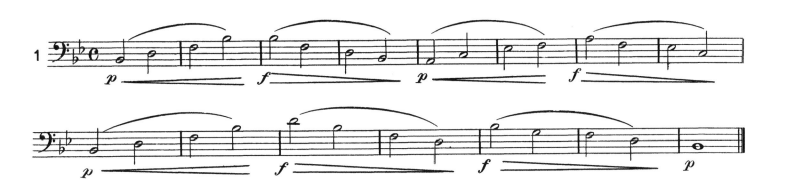

MELODY IN C

MELODY IN F

The Accent (Sforzando)

The accent or sforzando mark $>$ placed over or under a note indicates additional force is to be used. The degree of emphasis must be left to the good taste of the performer. Accents in soft music generally call for less additional emphasis than accents in loud music.

RECAPITULATION STUDY

Studies in Articulation

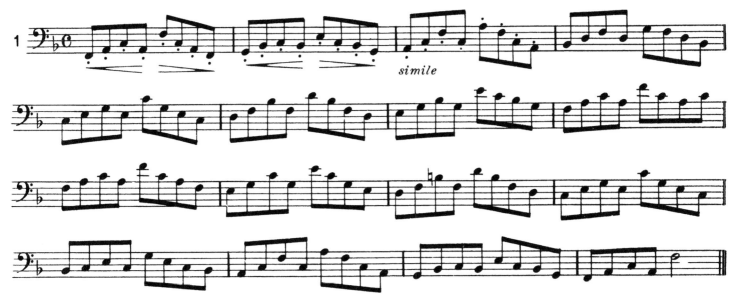

simile

Play the above exercise with the following articulations.

(a)　　　(b)　　　(c)　　　(d)

TRIPLET ARTICULATIONS

Slowly and carefully

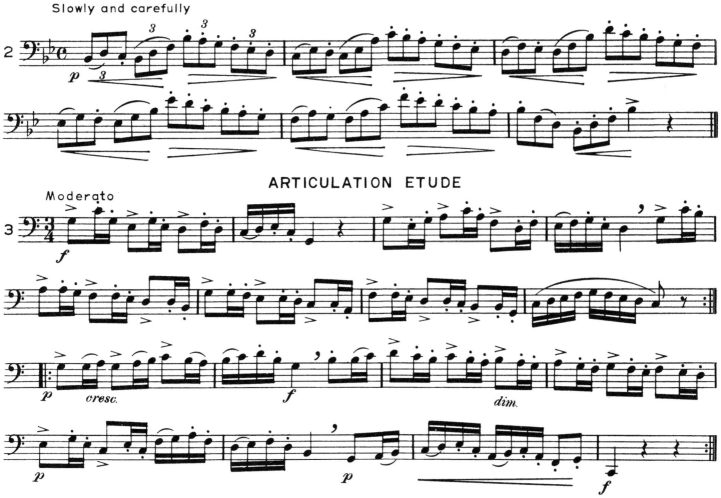

ARTICULATION ETUDE

Moderato

Studies in C Major

C Major Scale

Scale in Thirds– Use different articulations.

C Major Arpeggio– Use different articulations.

Play as rapidly as technic will permit.

Allegro moderato (moderately fast)

UPPER REGISTER REVIEW
(Check fingerings carefully)

SYNCOPATION IN 2/4

The Half-Staccato (Portamento)

The articulation indicated by 𝄐 has different names and interpretations. Modern usage, however, generally regards it as a form of *legato*, the nearest articulated approach to the slur. The student should attempt to play a *continuous tone* interrupted only by soft strokes of a *relaxed* tongue. The dot over the

last note of a slur is *not* a legato indication but a true staccato, thus

DOTTED EIGHTH NOTE REVIEW

SWEDISH MARCH

Preparatory Studies for A Minor

(Check fingerings carefully)

A MINOR SCALES

Harmonic Minor

Melodic Minor

A MINOR ETUDE

Adagio (very slowly)

Studies in F Major

F Major Scale

1

Scale in Thirds

2

F Major Arpeggio

3

Moderato

4

Allegro (quickly)

5

SYNCOPATION STUDY

D MINOR SCALES

Harmonic Minor

Melodic Minor

D MINOR ETUDE

breath accents-don't tongue

Studies in G Major

Tenor Clef

To avoid an **excessive** use of leger lines above the staff, music for the bassoon (particularly in orchestra, solos, and small ensemble) is frequently written in the tenor clef 𝄡. This clef indicates that middle C is found on the fourth line of the staff.

Duet in C Major

Studies in Bb Major

G MINOR SCALES

G MINOR ETUDE

CHORALE

Exercises for Acquiring a Fast Staccato

As rapidly as technic will permit. *Tongue lightly.*

Grace Notes

Grace notes are indicated by notes of a smaller size. There are two kinds, long and short. Long grace notes are no longer written by composers, but they occur very frequently in music written before the early 19th Century.

LONG GRACE NOTES

EXCERPT FROM SYMPHONY No. 12

HAYDN

SHORT GRACE NOTES

DOUBLE GRACE NOTES

CHROMATIC STUDY

Studies in D Major

D Major Scale

Scale in Thirds

ARPEGGIO STUDY

SYNCOPATION IN ¾ TIME

CHANGE OF CLEFS

Slowly

Play the eighth notes staccato, but with a *light* stroke of the tongue.

MOZART

B MINOR SCALES

Harmonic Minor

Melodic Minor

B MINOR ETUDE

Duet in B♭ Major

1 **Andante**

p cantabile (in a singing style)

mf

SYNCOPATION ACROSS THE BAR LINE

2 **Allegretto**

p

f

Fine

D.C. al Fine

TENOR CLEF STUDY

rfz (rinforzando) and *rf (rinforzo)* both mean reinforced or emphasized.

3 **Andante con moto**

p

rfz

p

f

marcato

rf ＞ p

Trills (tr⁓)

The *trill* (or shake) consists of the rapid alternation of two notes- the written one and the next one upward in the diatonic scale. Thus, a trill on A in the key of C will be from A to B; a trill on A in the key of F will be from A to Bb. An accidental placed above the trill sign indicates a trill to the note above modified by the accidental. The usual signs for the trill are *tr* and *tr⁓*.

In trills of sufficient length a special ending is used whether indicated or not, The closing of the trill consists of two tones: the scale tone below the written note and the written note itself unless altered by accidentals.

Refer to the Table of Trills, pages 26 to 29, for proper fingering in playing the following exercises.

Table of Trills for Bassoon (Heckel System)

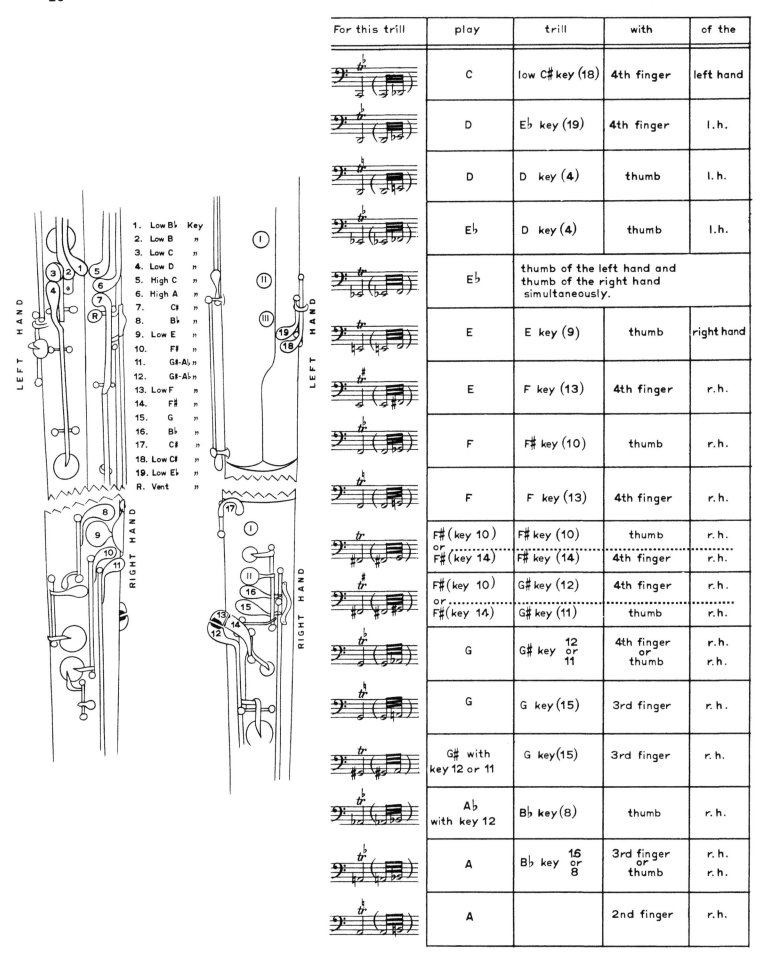

For this trill	play	trill	with	of the
	C	low C# key (18)	4th finger	left hand
	D	Eb key (19)	4th finger	l.h.
	D	D key (4)	thumb	l.h.
	Eb	D key (4)	thumb	l.h.
	Eb	thumb of the left hand and thumb of the right hand simultaneously.		
	E	E key (9)	thumb	right hand
	E	F key (13)	4th finger	r.h.
	F	F# key (10)	thumb	r.h.
	F	F key (13)	4th finger	r.h.
	F# (key 10) or F# (key 14)	F# key (10) — F# key (14)	thumb — 4th finger	r.h. — r.h.
	F# (key 10) or F# (key 14)	G# key (12) — G# key (11)	4th finger — thumb	r.h. — r.h.
	G	G# key 12 or 11	4th finger or thumb	r.h. r.h.
	G	G key (15)	3rd finger	r.h.
	G# with key 12 or 11	G key (15)	3rd finger	r.h.
	Ab with key 12	Bb key (8)	thumb	r.h.
	A	Bb key 16 or 8	3rd finger or thumb	r.h. r.h.
	A		2nd finger	r.h.

Key list:

1. Low Bb Key
2. Low B "
3. Low C "
4. Low D "
5. High C "
6. High A "
7. C# "
8. Bb "
9. Low E "
10. F# "
11. G#-Ab "
12. G#-Ab "
13. Low F "
14. F# "
15. G "
16. Bb "
17. C# "
18. Low C# "
19. Low Eb "
R. Vent "

LEFT HAND   RIGHT HAND

For this trill	play	trill		with	of the	Remarks
	B♭ with key 16 or key 8			2nd finger	r.h.	
	B♭ with key 16 or key 8			1st & 2nd fingers	r.h.	
	B			1st finger	r.h.	
	B			3rd finger	l.h.	
	C	C# key or	7 17	thumb or 1st finger	l.h. r.h.	
	C			3rd finger	l.h.	
	C# l.h. I II III r.h. C#(17)& F(13) keys			3rd finger	l.h.	
	D♭			3rd finger	l.h.	Addition of low D key(4) to D♭ fingering may be desirable.
	D	C# key (7)		thumb	l.h.	
	D			2nd finger	l.h.	
	D# r.h. I III			3rd finger	l.h.	Addition of E♭ key (19) may be desirable.
	E l.h. II III r.h. II G (15) key			2nd & 3rd fingers	l.h.	or I II l.h. C# key (7) and trill C# key(7)
	E			1st finger	l.h.	
	E l.h. II r.h. G(15)& F(13)keys			1st & 2nd fingers	r.h.	On some bassoons it is better to use l.h. I instead of l.h. II.
	F r.h. G (15) & F (13) keys			1st & 2nd fingers	r.h.	
	F r.h. I II and G (15) key			2nd & 3rd fingers	l.h.	
	F# with key 10	F# key (10)		thumb	r.h.	Or play F# key(14) and trill key 14.

For this trill	play	trill	with the	of the	Remarks
[musical notation]	F♯ with key 14	G♯ key (11)			Or play F♯ with key 10 and trill G♯ key 12
[musical notation]	G	A♭ key 12 or 11	4th finger or thumb	r.h. r.h.	
[musical notation]	G	G key (15)	3rd finger	r.h.	
[musical notation]	G♯ with key 12 or key 11	G key (15)	3rd finger	r.h.	
[musical notation]	A♭ with key 12	B♭ key (8)	thumb	r.h.	
[musical notation]	A	B♭ key (16 or 8)	3rd finger or thumb	r.h.	
[musical notation]	A		2nd finger	r.h.	
[musical notation]	B♭ with key 16 or key 8		2nd finger	r.h.	
[musical notation]	B♭ with key 16 or key 8		1st and 2nd fingers	r.h.	
[musical notation]	B		1st finger	r.h.	
[musical notation]	B		3rd finger	l.h.	
[musical notation]	C	C♯ key 7 or 17	thumb or 1st finger	l.h. r.h.	
[musical notation]	C		3rd finger	l.h.	
[musical notation]	C♯ l.h. I II III r.h. II G(15) & F(13)		3rd finger	l.h.	
[musical notation]	D♭ with II G key (15) and F key (13) r.h.		3rd or 1st finger	l.h.	
[musical notation]	D	G key (15) or C♯ key (7)	3rd finger or thumb	r.h. l.h.	With 1st trill fingering (key 15) it may be desirable to also trill II r.h.
[musical notation]	D		2nd finger	l.h.	

For this trill	play	trill	with the	of the	Remarks
(notation)	D#		2nd finger	l.h.	or l.h. I II C# key (7) trill: l.h. II
(notation)	Eb		1st and 2nd fingers	l.h.	
(notation)	E	G key (15)	3rd finger	r.h.	
(notation)	E	G key (15) and	2nd finger	r.h.	
(notation)	F		2nd finger	r.h.	
(notation)	F l.h. II III r.h. I II Ab key (12)		1st and 2nd fingers	r.h.	or if bassoon has high G trill key, finger F regular way and use trill key.
(notation)	F#	F key (13)	4th finger	r.h.	
(notation)	F#	G key (15)	3rd finger	r.h.	
(notation)	G	C# and A keys (7 and 6)	thumb	l.h.	Use one half hole I l.h. if necessary.
(notation)	G	C# and A keys (7 and 6)	thumb	l.h.	At beginning of trill let go right hand I and F key (13).
(notation)	G#	C# and A keys (7 and 6)	thumb	l.h.	
(notation)	A with low D (4)		3rd finger	l.h.	
(notation)	A use F key (13) instead of G key (15)	Trill r.h. II closed l.h. III open and so on alternately			
(notation)	Bb		3rd finger	l.h.	
(notation)	B		2nd finger	l.h.	
(notation)	C		3rd finger	l.h.	On some bassoons trill III r.h. and G key (15) simultaneously.
(notation)	C#		1st finger	l.h.	

Studies in E♭ Major

MAGIC FLUTE OVERTURE
(Orchestral Excerpt)

MOZART

C MINOR SCALES

C MINOR ETUDE

STUDY IN 12/8 TIME

Allegretto (in 4)

ETUDE IN BASS AND TENOR CLEFS

Andantino

CHROMATIC STUDY

Practice slowly

The Turn (Gruppetto)

The turn ∾ consists of four tones: the next scale tone above the written tone, the written tone itself, the tone below the written tone, and the written tone again. The examples illustrate only some of the interpretations and problems of the turn.

GRUPPETTO STUDY

STUDY IN ORNAMENTATION

Studies in A Major

A MIDSUMMER NIGHT'S DREAM
(Orchestral Excerpt)

Practice also with trill fingering for high F#.

Allegro molto comodo

MENDELSSOHN

F# MINOR SCALES

Harmonic Minor

Melodic Minor

F# MINOR ETUDE

Slowly

(1) ✗ is the symbol for the double sharp; f double sharp = G♮.

Studies in A♭ Major

TRIPLET STUDY

F MINOR SCALES

F MINOR ETUDE

Studies in E Major

E Major Scale

Scale in Thirds

E Major Arpeggio

Allegretto grazioso

Tempo di Valse moderato

C♯ MINOR SCALES

Harmonic Minor

1

Melodic Minor

2

C♯ MINOR ETUDES

Allegretto

3

Andante con moto

4

Fine p dolce

D.C. al Fine

Advanced Scales

CHROMATIC ETUDE

1073-39